Pocahontas

by Joanne Mattern

Content Consultant
Nanci R. Vargus, Ed.D.
Professor Emeritus, University of Indianapolis

Reading Consultant
Jeanne M. Clidas, Ph.D.
Reading Specialist

Children's Press®
An Imprint of Scholastic Inc.
New York Toronto London Auckland Sydney
Mexico City New Delhi Hong Kong
Danbury, Connecticut

Library of Congress Cataloging-in-Publication Data
Mattern, Joanne, 1963-
   Pocahontas/by Joanne Mattern; poem by Jodie Shepherd.
      pages cm. — (Rookie biographies)
   Includes bibliographical references index.
   Audience: Ages 3-6.
   ISBN 978-0-531-20596-9 (library binding)— 978-0-531-20998-1 (pbk.)
1. Pocahontas, -1617—Juvenile literature. 2. Powhatan women—Biography—Juvenile
literature. 3. Jamestown (Va.)—History—Juvenile literature. 4. Virginia—History—
Colonial period, ca. 1600-1775—Juvenile literature. I. Shepherd, Jodie. II. Title.

E99.P85M38 2015
975.501092—dc23 [B]   2014035675

Produced by Spooky Cheetah Press
Poem by Jodie Shepherd
Design by Keith Plechaty

Printed in China 62

SCHOLASTIC, CHILDREN'S PRESS, ROOKIE BIOGRAPHIES®, and associated logos
are trademarks and/or registered trademarks of Scholastic Inc.

4 5 6 7 8 9 10 R 24 23 22 21 20 19 18 17

Photographs ©: Dreamstime/Teresa Kenney: 3 top right; Getty Images: 3 top
left (Marilyn Angel Wynn), 16 (MPI), 31 center top, 31 center bottom; iStockphoto/
chpaquette: 28; Jamestown Settlement History Museum, Williamsburg, VA: 8;
National Geographic Creative/W. Langdon Kihn: cover inset, 4, 30 left; North Wind
Picture Archives: 11, 31 top; Shutterstock, Inc./eurobanks: 3 bottom; Superstock, Inc.:
19 (Universal Images Group), 12; The Image Works: cover (The Print Collector/HIP),
27 (Mary Evans), 23, 24, 30 right (North Wind Picture Archives); Thinkstock/Peter
Dennis: 15, 20, 31 bottom.

Map by XNR Productions, Inc.

Table of Contents

Meet Pocahontas

Pocahontas was an American Indian girl. Without her help, the early English **settlers** at Jamestown might have died. She was one of America's earliest heroes.

FAST FACT!

"Pocahontas" was a nickname that meant "playful one."

Pocahontas was born around 1595 in what is now known as Virginia. Her real name was Matoaka (muh-TOH-uh-kuh). Her father was a chief named Powhatan (pow-HAT-uhn). Powhatan ruled about 30 tribes in Virginia. Pocahontas was his favorite child.

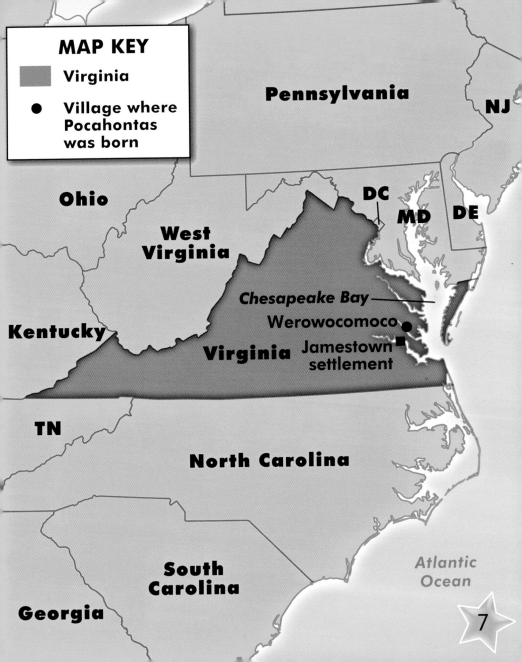

MAP KEY

Virginia

● Village where Pocahontas was born

Pennsylvania

NJ

Ohio

DC

MD

DE

West Virginia

Chesapeake Bay

Werowocomoco

Kentucky

Virginia

Jamestown settlement

TN

North Carolina

South Carolina

Atlantic Ocean

Georgia

7

As a young girl, Pocahontas grew crops and gathered plants and seeds to eat. She helped the women prepare food and build houses. Pocahontas probably never saw anyone who was not Indian like her. Then, when Pocahontas was about 11 years old, everything changed.

This photo shows what Pocahontas's village would have looked like.

Strangers Arrive

In spring of 1607, English settlers came to Virginia and built a town named Jamestown. Their leader was Captain John Smith. One day, some of Powhatan's warriors captured Smith. They brought him back to the chief's village.

Early meetings between the Indians and the English were not friendly.

Powhatan ordered his men to make Smith lie on the ground. They placed his head on a rock. One of the warriors went to hit Smith with a club. Suddenly, Pocahontas ran over. She put her head down over Smith's head. Powhatan told his warriors not to kill Smith.

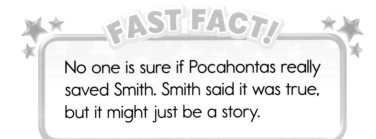

FAST FACT!

No one is sure if Pocahontas really saved Smith. Smith said it was true, but it might just be a story.

After Smith's scary experience, the Indians and the English became friendlier. They visited each other and **traded** goods. The Indians would bring food and the English would give them metal pots, beads, and axes in return.

Without food from the Indians, the settlers would have starved.

Life got harder for the English settlers. They did not know what plants to grow in America. They were **starving**. Powhatan helped by sending them food. Pocahontas often brought these gifts to the English. She grew close to the people at Jamestown.

This shows what the Jamestown settlement looked like.

Captured!

As the English grew hungrier, they demanded that Powhatan give them more food and supplies. The chief wanted weapons in exchange for food. John Smith said no. Powhatan refused to help the English.

Smith did not want the Indians to have weapons.

One day, Smith got hurt. He had to go back to England. The new leader of Jamestown came up with a plan to make Powhatan give him food. He tricked Pocahontas into coming onto his ship. Then he would not let her leave.

Pocahontas was a prisoner at Jamestown for one year. During that time, she learned to speak English. She dressed in English clothes and learned English **customs**. In 1614, she married an Englishman named John Rolfe.

FAST FACT!

While she lived with the English, Pocahontas changed her name to Rebecca.

23

Peace of Pocahontas

Pocahontas and Rolfe had a son named Thomas. There was peace among the people again. In 1616, the leaders at Jamestown sent Pocahontas and her family to England. They wanted to show how the English and Indians could live peacefully together.

This is a painting of Pocahontas and her son, Thomas.

Pocahontas was treated well in England. She met the king and queen. People called her a princess. But when the Rolfes were ready to come home, Pocahontas got very sick. She died in England at 21 years old.

Here, Pocahontas is meeting James I, King of England.

Timeline of Pocahontas's Life

1613
captured by the English

1595
born in Virginia

1607
English settlers arrive in Virginia

Pocahontas accomplished a lot in her short life. Thanks to her help, Jamestown became a successful settlement. She helped the English understand how to survive in America. She also showed how people from different cultures could be friends.

1616
sails to England

1614
marries John Rolfe

1617
dies in March

A Poem About Pocahontas

Did this story really happen?
Did Pocahontas save the captain?
Here is what we know is true:
Her tribe helped get the settlers through,
and little by little, friendship grew.

You Can Be a Peacemaker

- Be kind to people who are different from you.

- Help people in need.

- Do your best to understand other people's points of view.

Glossary

customs (KUSS-tums): the way a group of people act and think

settlers (SET-lurs): people who come to a new place to live

starving (STAR-ving): not having enough food

traded (TRAYD-ed): exchanged one thing for another

Index

Facts for Now

Visit this Scholastic Web site for more information on Pocahontas:
www.factsfornow.scholastic.com
Enter the keyword **Pocahontas**

About the Author

Joanne Mattern has written more than 250 books for children. She especially likes writing biographies because she loves to learn about real people and the things they do. Joanne also enjoys writing about science, nature, and history. She grew up in New York State and still lives there with her husband, four children, and several pets.